MURDER AND MYSTERY
IN DEVON

by Judy Chard

Best wishes
Judy Chard

Acknowledgements for illustrations:

Luxton Tragedy - Judy Chard.

Laura Dimes Mystery - Judy Chard.

Babbacombe Lee by kind permission of Devon and Cornwall Constabulary.

Salcombe's Dark Mystery - Peter Burke.

Maye Murder Mystery - Judy Chard.

Warcombe Farm Tragedy - Artist's impression taken from supplement to "*Kingsbridge Journal*" and "*Salcombe Times*", 18th June 1904.

First Published in Great Britain in 1994

Copyright © Judy Chard

ISBN 1 898964 10 6

Orchard Publications
2 Orchard Close, Chudleigh, Newton Abbot, Devon TQ13 0LR
Telephone (01626) 852714

Designed, Typeset and Printed for Orchard Publications by
Swift Print, 2 High Street, Dawlish, Devon EX7 9HP

CONTENTS

The Luxton Tragedy - September 1975
The Farm Where Time Stood Still ......

A learned man once said "What do they know of England who do not know Devon?", but the trouble is many people who think they know the county, do not. They think of it as a gentle, soft, idyllic area – what they do not realise is that under this appearance seethes the same cauldron of mystery, murder, human weakness, emotion and passion as in all parts of the world.

Many parts of Devon remain unknown at heart, out of the mists of the moors and coombes come some of the strangest unsolved murders ever recounted. But a shadow that once falls on a·wall leaves a shadow there forever – and so it is with an unsolved murder.

The most chilling factor of this tragedy is the setting on a remote farm near Winkleigh in mid Devon – West Chapple.

West Chapple Farm

The three people who lived there had existed in a virtual Victorian time warp which ended when their dead bodies were found, each blasted through the head with a double barrelled shot gun – the first, that of Alan Luxton.

The farm was owned and run by Robbie and Alan Luxton and their sister, Frances. They had all been born on the farm. When they died they were aged 65, 53 and 68 respectively. The driver of a grocery delivery van, arriving at the farm on a September morning in 1975 found the place apparently deserted, except for a dog barking from the barn where it had obviously been shut in. He knocked on the back door and receiving no answer, went across the yard. It was then he saw what he thought was a bundle of rags above which hovered a cloud of flies.

It was the body of Alan Luxton. He was dressed only in pyjamas and army boots. The top part of his head was missing and his brains and part of his skull were scattered far and wide. He was lying in a pool of blood but there did not seem to be any weapon near him.

In a state of shock, the driver fled to Winkleigh to tell the police what he had seen. Within an hour Detective Chief Superintendent Proven Sharpe had set up investigations and a forensic expert was brought by helicopter from Bristol. Obviously the killer could still be at large so the police had to "Proceed with caution." As they moved around the garden they discovered further evidence of death – flesh, bones, brains, all scattered in the garden, the orchard and farmyard. The house itself appeared to be locked and although the police eventually broke in through a window, there was no sign of the other two members of the family – Robbie and Frances.

At last with further searching PC Tilke found their corpses lying half hidden in the long grass among the rotting apples in the orchard. Frances had her night-gown pushed above her waist and was lying half on her side, the top of her head missing. Robbie wore a vest, trousers and boots similar to his brother. His injuries were also to his head. By his side lay a shotgun, the kind kept by most farmers for shooting rabbits.

The farm labourer, Fred Lyne, who had been with the family for many years, identified the bodies. Although he had seen the grocery van speeding back along the lane, he claimed he had not known anything was wrong.

The Luxtons were the last surviving members of a once famous, rich, and widespread Devon family going back to the 14th century – landowners, riders to hounds – and gamblers; these last three members were more or less complete recluses by the year 1975, in fact Alan had not been seen outside the farm gates for 20 years.

They still farmed with 19th century methods, outdated machinery and cobbled yards. They used scythes and prangs or pitchforks to turn their hay. Their corn stood in stooks and they layered their hedges immaculately by hand, all as in days of old when labour was cheap and machinery mostly non-existent and no one had heard of the ubiquitous hedge trimmer or bulldozer. They had no electricity or mains water; an enormous iron wheel motivated the Victorian machinery for power – such as there was; lighting was by paraffin lamp and candle.

Now rumours and gossip were rife. It was an obvious case of murder and then suicide, no outsider was involved in their death as few had been in their lives. There were hints of mental disorder. In all the newspapers every account by journalists was written from a different angle making fantasy reading. Many stressed the point that country life as assessed by the "townie" or "grockle" was meant to be idyllic and even more so in this case as it had not been polluted by modern machinery, concrete, fertilisers, weed killers et al. Life should have been perfect so why this horrific end?

The Devon countryside, as already stated, specially in Mid Devon, is secretive with deep hidden lanes, it hugs itself and its people to itself. It is really only comparatively recently that easy access has come to the area which could easily become cut off by blizzards, flood, gales, fallen trees, narrow lanes blocked and impassable. Families were thrown on their own reserves and resources, and even for marriage, often their own kin – close knit.

The gossip spread, people talked of course. It seems that West Chapple Farm had been up for sale for six months, but the family blew hot and cold, the brothers had even come to blows over the matter. Frances and Robbie were anxious to sell, Alan was not. They kept changing their minds, as they had over buying a house in Crediton where they had dithered to such an extent the vendor had got fed up and terminated the whole matter.

Some people muttered about their meanness, their non-socialising, the way they were against progress of any kind. The way Frances seemed to haunt the local graveyards including Brushford, studying her ancestors ... some even said incest ran in the family, as it was always suspected it did in many of the old Devon families; this would account for the mental state of these three, particularly Alan. Some of the villagers 'had their own ideas about Frances and Robbie'.

During the inquest Fred Lyne, the labourer who had worked for them for so many years, said he took his orders from Robert whom he considered to be "the Maister". He described how Alan walked around with just a sack tied round his waist, he seemed to vary between madness and sanity. He said soon after the discussion over selling the house had come up, one day when he was working outside Frances called him into the kitchen. He saw Alan had a double barrelled shotgun in his hands. He suggested to Robert that he take the gun off his brother, and that the cartridges should be hidden.

Fred was not the only man working for the Luxtons – a man called Boroweiz, a Ukrainian refugee had come to Britain after the war, and now he and his wife lived in a tied cottage on the farm, glad of the comparative remoteness. Like Fred, he had been given a week's notice before the shootings. He said his wife worked sometimes in the house for Frances.

Mrs Boroweiz gave evidence saying she had often heard quarrelling and felt sure Alan was mental. She added that she was "never allowed upstairs in the bedrooms where the three of them slept," as far as she was concerned with the cleaning it was "downstairs only."

It seems Frances had wanted to make a home for her brother at this house in Crediton and Robbie would have been willing, the farm had become too much, they were always short of money, but Alan would have none of it and said if they went he would stay on the farm alone, which was of course ridiculous.

Lute House where the farm worker lived

As a Devonian I realise we are not on the whole easy people to get to know, although having lived and worked outside the county perhaps I see things from a different angle, but I can quite easily understand how these three felt when the farm had been in the family for generations. They had worked themselves to the bone to keep their home, and now it was getting impossible to work, added to which was what we perhaps would call congenital weaknesses, at least in one

5

member of the family. Alan had had a love affair in his youth with a girl from Hatherleigh called Myrtle, it was said she was very beautiful and he was deeply in love, but suddenly for no reason that anyone knows, this was broken off and he became distraught. Perhaps this just helped to tip him over the tenuous line between complete sanity and being a little mental, a state which exists in most of us.

Frances, like many people today, was almost obsessively interested in her family history – it is both sad and ironic that there were no Luxtons at the funeral, only some members of her mother's family, the Short's.

At one time Alan had been quite the young blood, member of the Young Farmers, he drank and smoked at the Kings Arms and even at one time he had wanted to sell up his part of the farm and start up on his own, but at that time the other two would have none of it.

Like many Devonian families, there was a history of cousins marrying cousins, often to keep money in the family, their motto 'You cannot take out more than you put in.'

Frances is an enigma too; at one time she had travelled abroad and even had a brief affair with a Dutch seaman she met when staying with a friend in London – one can't help wondering what he thought of the family if he ever met them.

As elsewhere, the second world war brought many changes even to West Chapple and Winkleigh. In 1940 some cockneys were billeted at Lute House on the farm. In 1942 the United States Airforce built an airfield to prepare for D-Day, and Alan was still young enough to enjoy himself with the Yanks. He probably smoked their cigarettes and drank with them at the Kings Arms. In 1944 the Yanks left and the Canadians arrived, their Lynx squadron flying sorties to the Brest Peninsular. Gossip had it that Frances was 'carrying on' with one of the airmen, although there is no information as to where or how, or even whether they really met.

At the inquest the Coroner was Col. D F Brown, William Kennard was the Home Office Pathologist and he gave detailed evidence regarding the gun and the lurid facts about Alan's brains, which were more widely scattered than Robbie's. His explanation for this was that in the farming community suicides, of which it seems there are many, favoured the centre of the forehead for their target where the humane killer in cattle is directed, so that with Alan the gun was closer to the head than in either Robbie's or Frances's case. The evidence proved that he had died first, then Frances and Robbie last of all. Det. Chief Superintendent Proven Sharpe described the scene the police had found immediately after the shootings. A stick was found near Alan's right hand – he said this was typical of a suicide with a long barrelled shotgun – it seems that shotgun killings and incest on lonely farms were his speciality! Beside Robbie's leg was a double barrelled shotgun and also a short stick, and live and spent cartridges in his pocket. There had been no sign of any struggle and he concluded that Alan took his own life first, it was difficult to ascertain when exactly Frances had been shot. Robbie had committed suicide – the woman had definitely not killed herself ... none of the victims had struggled – bloodstains had blurred the fingerprints so perhaps Robbie and Frances had heard Alan shoot himself, which had been threatened for so long, they had rushed out into the yard and found him, and in the state of mind they were already in, Robbie shot his sister – either with or without her consent – and then turned the gun on himself. So – the verdict – Mr Alan Luxton committed suicide, Mr Robert Luxton killed his sister and then himself committed suicide.

None of us will ever know exactly what happened, or can imagine the agony of mind they suffered on that mild, September morning underneath the apple trees, heavy with fruit, trees that had produced cider for the family down the generations and now at whose feet lay the bodies of the last of the Luxton family among the fly blown, rotting apples.

West Chapple Farmhouse and yard

The Mysterious Affair of Laura Dimes
April 1884

The ivy-clad ruins of the mansion of Oldstone at Blackawton in the South Hams would make a wonderful backcloth for a haunted horror film, and some years ago when I talked to Graham Andrew who, with his brother Brian, farmed here he told me some of the tragedies that occurred here in Victorian times, the most strange and horrific of all – the death of Laura Dimes, still unexplained.

The farmhouse itself dates back to Saxon times, a courthouse stood here, the basis of the building which is now Oldstone Farm, and it feels as if a tragic shadow still hangs over it, a haunting of its hollow former glory. In the 18th century a block with a Georgian front and Tuscan doorway was added, now it stands empty, a smoke stained shell filled with nettles and rubbish.

All that is left of Oldstone Mansion

The Dimes family lived here from 1839 into the 1970s, typical of a prosperous Victorian family, living in the traditional splendour of the period and employing many people from the village, on the estate. Then suddenly in the 1880s it was as if some curse fell upon them, disasters occurred to destroy this idyllic life.

The whole atmosphere of the place is eerie, a kind of supernatural aura pervades it, fostered by underground passages with spy-hole slits, parts of which can be glanced through grids, mostly blocked by cave ins. Were they once a means of escape – and if so, for whom and from what?

In a nearby wood there is a stone built structure, a kind of folly where a hermit lived. This was the age of Capability Brown when it was the fashion to have grottoes and follies and to invite hermits to live on the premises or estate. This building would have been his larder where food would be brought from the house. Lower down by a pond is the hermitage itself, later used as a boathouse.

There is also a shell house, another popular kind of gazebo where the ladies of the house and their visitors could sit and sip their tea on hot afternoons. Once the walls were covered with shells stuck on with mortar, reminiscent of La Ronde near Exmouth. In this case many were removed by the GIs as souvenirs during the war when they were stationed in the South Hams for rehearsals on Slapton beach for D-Day.

I am not at all surprised that the historian Hoskins described Oldstone as "Dark and melancholy among the chestnuts, nettles and the elder."

The woods in which the hermit's cell stands are part of a dell with trees running down to three ponds or ornamental lakes feeding each other. These woods are now part of the Woodland Leisure Park run by the Bendall family, who reconstructed the original scene by damming the top pond.

When I first visited the site in the early 1980s, the woods were overgrown and I found them lonely, even sinister where no birds sang, haunted by the tragedy of Laura Dimes' mysterious death as a young bride of only a few weeks after she married Hugh Shortland.

Her body was found upright with her hat still on her head, was she murdered or was it suicide? If the former, who was the murderer? It was an April day in 1884 when her body was found, it was also April nearly one hundred years later when I stood looking at the murky water, the day hot and still, the spot twilit with growth and wildness. And no wonder it felt thus for the story connected with it is bizarre in the extreme, and in a letter from Mrs Ursula Khan, nee Dimes of Blackawton, which she kindly wrote me in 1985. she related the true story of her great Aunt Laura Dimes saying "It is true in every detail. . ."

Her great Aunt Laura Constantia Dimes was born in 1861, one of three daughters and a son born to Martha and William Dimes of Oldstone, Blackawton. She was both beautiful and talented and led the life of a daughter of a rich man, sheltered, luxurious. She often rode to hounds, always accompanied by her groom. However on one particular occasion when she was 24 years old for some reason she had gone out on her own and it was then she met Hugh Rutherford Shortland aged 25 – the son of a doctor who had once been secretary to Sir George Grey, the Governor of New Zealand. Although she did not know it, Hugh was involved in some rather questionable mining deals, he had an office of some kind at Mallet's Hotel in Ivybridge.

Laura fell head over heels in love with this dashing young blade. He seems to have been a man of some mystery and more than likely a fortune hunter. Laura would of course have been a good catch with her rich parents; rather naturally they disapproved of this casual friendship and eventually this drove Hugh and Laura to obtain a special licence so they could get married, which they did at Kingsbridge Register Office on 8 April 1884. It seems that Laura had ridden out in the morning as usual and she must have either been accompanied by her

11

Tuscany Gate in ruins of Oldstone Mansion

groom, or else have sworn him to secrecy – she was married rather unglamorously, in her riding habit – unglamorously but perhaps romantic.

For some reason Hugh then said he had to leave immediately for New Zealand as he already had a business appointment from which he could not escape, so he returned to Ivybridge to arrange his trip while Laura went home to Oldstone where she broke the news to her parents.

History doesn't relate what exactly took place but it doesn't need much imagination to assume they had to accept the fait accompli albeit, unwillingly. It is more than likely her mother would be more lenient in her reaction.

The couple had been married less than three weeks – the bride went out on her usual morning ride on 25 April whilst of course everyone presumed Hugh was on his way to New Zealand and would return as soon as possible. Laura returned to the house shortly before noon and changed from her riding clothes into a dress and straw hat and took her collie dog into the woods for a walk, this was nothing unusual. From that walk she never returned. It seems strange that her absence from the house at lunch and all afternoon and evening did not surprise her parents.

Mrs Dimes said at the inquest that she simply thought Laura had gone to meet her husband in reply to a letter she had received and added that if he had had to defer his journey then this was quite possible. Eventually Mrs Dimes did go down to Oldstone woods thinking that she might meet her daughter and son-in-law walking there, all of which strikes me as extraordinary because where did she imagine they had been all night, and also what had become of the dog? Surely it would have returned to the house alone and this would have aroused suspicion. There is no record anywhere of anyone having commented on these curious circumstances. Anyway Mrs Dimes saw nothing and went back to the house, it was only as a result of the curiosity of Elizabeth Luckraft, wife of the hind, or steward, of the estate which led her to find Laura's body.

She was in the habit of taking her own dog for a swim in one of the ponds and there she saw a woman's hat a few inches under water about three feet out from the bank. On looking closer she saw a face and figure beneath it. She ran in horrified haste to fetch help from a farm labourer. When they took the body from the water they saw it was Laura Shortland. She had been standing on the bed of the pond, one hand stretched out in front of her, the water just covering the top of her hat.

The police were called immediately and an inquest arranged. Giving evidence, Sergeant Mills of Blackawton said Laura Dimes, now Shortland, was fully dressed and her clothing gave no evidence of a struggle of any kind, nor did it seem she had made any effort to get out of the water. The depth of the pond at this point was 6ft 3ins. They had discovered a small bruise on her temple, so slight that it had almost disappeared when the jury saw the body and he had no reason to suspect foul play.

From this point the whole situation gets curiouser and curiouser. On the day of her death it was true a letter had arrived from Hugh, her husband. It had been forwarded by his solicitor in Plymouth and dated from Brindisi. Apart from the fact that he said he was on the way home there doesn't seem to be any further details of what was in the letter. He had all his correspondence sent to Mallet's Hotel in Ivybridge, mostly of a business nature. On Friday 2 May a young man named Ryder called to ask for any correspondence which might have arrived for Hugh Shortland. He was treated by the management with some suspicion as Shortland was meant to be in New Zealand, so Ryder left, whether with or without the correspondence we do not know.

Ryder was an old friend of Hugh's; he lived in Modbury with his father who had a small cottage inside the yard of the tannery where he worked, a secluded spot well away from the public eye. Here Shortland stayed from time to time. As a result of this call at the hotel, reported to the police, they became suspicious and went to the cottage to question him. Ryder said he had last actually seen Shortland in Modbury when he was leaving for Brindisi on his way to New Zealand.

At 9am on 7 May Ryder's father went to the police and told them Shortland was at the cottage. PC Dunsford then arrested Shortland on a charge of murdering his wife. At the time young Ryder was in Plymouth where he worked. They sent for him and lay in wait just inside the yard of the tannery, caught him and charged him with being an accomplice in the murder of Laura Shortland. Subsequent enquiries showed that Hugh had never been to Brindisi, in fact he had never left Modbury.

The pool where Laura drowned, now marked as
Dangerous - Deep water

Two days after the wedding, on 10 April, he had gone to Ryder's cottage in the dark, before his wife's death, and stayed there until he was arrested on 7 May. if this story was true and Shortland had been hidden there since 10 April to 7 May he could not have murdered his wife who died on 25 April.

He was taken before Mr W R Ilbert at Kingsbridge Court and charged with murdering his wife. Ryder was also brought up and charged with aiding and abetting in the murder, but of course the police had no shred of evidence against either of them and the case had to be dismissed. Scotland Yard was called in, Laura's body was exhumed, long proceedings ensued but once again the case collapsed for lack of evidence and the whole thing became a complete mystery.

In her letter Mrs Khan (Ursula Dimes) told me her own theory of the unsolved mystery.

"Let us assume that Shortland had asked Laura for money due to some trouble he was in and arranged an assignment to meet him in the woods to hand it over, either to himself or this friend, Ryder. Laura might possibly have confided the circumstances to her mother, even perhaps borrowed money from her, consequently Mrs Dimes didn't worry too much when her daughter didn't return to the house for lunch and later assumed she had gone away with him. But did Laura and Hugh quarrel over money, when she found he was engaged in some underhand, perhaps even criminal, matter, did she commit suicide? Or was she reluctant to hand over the money when she found the real reason he needed it.

If it was Ryder who came for it, did he have trouble in getting it from her and strike her on the temple, hence the bruise, then turning round and beating a hasty retreat as she slipped in the mud on the edge of the pond, fell into the water and her feet became stuck in the mud as if in a bog as she struggled to get out. Perhaps whichever of the two came to meet her, neither realised what had happened and that she was drowning.

The other solution – suicide – is most unlikely in a girl brought up like Laura was, newly married and deeply in love. Admitted she could have been genuinely shocked and deeply upset that he had lied about going to New Zealand and also at his criminal activities, if that is what they were.

As regards Shortland, he would have been deeply shocked when he heard the news of his wife's death, hiding until the inquest was over made it look more than ever as if he was guilty but probably he acted. on the spur of the moment, particularly if he was in some kind of money trouble already."

However we have to remember that when Shortland returned to New Zealand later, he served a prison sentence for debt.

My own possible solution is that she found out he was in debt and she herself threatened to go to the police. Who knows? It is certain that with a girl like that, one who in those days would be described as "delicately nurtured" to find herself bound irrevocably to a criminal could have been a traumatic shock, but arguments have been going to and fro ever since and probably will do into the mists of time.

Laura's mother died a year later, more than likely of a broken heart, and six years later her father followed his wife. His son took over the house in 1891 and in February 1895 the Western Morning News reported that the family mansion of Oldstone had been destroyed by one of the worst fires in the district in living memory. It had started at 5pm on a Saturday night when the kitchen chimney caught fire. Mr Dimes got his wife and children out of the house, but the fire spread rapidly and was soon a mass of flames, the floors fell in, the whole conflagration fanned by a strong east wind, only the outside walls remained standing. It had been the worst winter in living memory and all the water pipes were frozen, the lanes piled high with snow and impassable so no fire engine could come from Dartmouth and it was useless for the farm hands and villagers to form a chain of buckets as there was no water to fill them. They removed as much of the furniture and antiques as they could.

Another curious aspect added to all this is the fact that one room retained its walls and windows uncracked. This was the room where it was said a little chimney sweep had once been locked in as a prank by young members of the Dimess family and had screamed to be let out because he saw "something" high up on the wall of the room. Perhaps an image of poor drowned Laura.

There are other various ghost stories with the usual headless horses, and even an apparition which walks daily under the archway leading from the house – at midnight and noon.

Who knows what the ghosts of years past have left in such a place, but as Ursula Dimes says in her book, "I would not care to test them in such settings."

Nor would I

She has written a first class booklet *"Oldstone: The Story of a Ruined Mansion"* which is a picture of a typical South Hams family down the years, researched in great detail, obtainable from Dartmouth Museum or the Harbour Book Shop in Dartmouth.

Oldstone Farmhouse today

The Man They Couldn't Hang - 1884
John Henry George Lee – "Babbacombe" Lee

This is perhaps the most macabre and the most famous murder case of all time because it became even more prominent after the occurrence than during the trial itself. Three times they attempted to hang John Henry George Lee known as "Babbacombe" Lee, and three times they failed, it was said, thus proving his innocence.

It is true that no satisfactory solution has ever been found as to how John Lee managed to elude the death sentence passed on him for the murder of Miss Emma Keyse. The whole story is full of unsolved mysteries and explanations, all of which prove unsatisfactory. Although he was accused of the murder of this woman, his employer, he had no real motive sufficient to incur murder; she had shown him nothing but kindness and tolerance for years, and probably today, for this reason, he would have been judged innocent.

Born in 1864 he came from a very respectable family and lived with his widowed mother at 3, Town Cottages in Abbotskerswell near Newton Abbot. At the age of 15 he went to work for Miss Emma Keyse in her thatched house, The Glen, Beach Road, Babbacombe, Torquay. In her younger days she had been to Court as maid of honour to Queen Victoria and hobnobbed with the highest in the lands; a lady of great distinction, rich, kind, and well loved in the society of St. Marychurch and Babbacombe.

Lee worked for her for 18 months; then perhaps the gentle lap of the sea against the garden wall, the sight of the big ships passing on the horizon, and the tales of the local fishermen, had an effect on him for he joined the Royal Navy – much against the will of his family as he had a weak chest. They were proved right for the tough life was too much for him, he developed pneumonia and to his great disappointment, was invalided out. He had won a "Progress" Prize and was getting on well, so perhaps this set back affected and soured him, perhaps the rest of the horrifying story might not have occurred if he had been able to carry on with his chosen career.

He got a job at the Yacht Club Hotel, after that as a porter at Torre Station, finally with Colonel Brownlow. Now he was foolish enough to steal silver from his employer and was sent to Exeter prison in July 1883 for six months. Emma Keyse had kept in touch with him and she wrote to the Governor saying she would give him a job and be responsible for him. At that time the household of The Glen consisted of two elderly servants, Eliza and Jane Neck, and the cook, Elizabeth Harris who, although no one seemed to know at the time, was pregnant. Lee was her half brother and she had added her plea to Emma on his behalf.

The Glen as it was in 1885

For three months all went well. Then Lee started to get lazy and discontented. Miss Keyse put up with it as long as she could, but at last she reduced his wages from 2/6d a week to 2/- until he mended his way. This was in October and it made Lee more difficult than ever, he was seething with annoyance, although he didn't show it to his employer at the time. On the night of 15 November when Miss Keyse had drunk the cocoa that Jane Neck had brought her, she went into the hall, presumably to go to bed, but she never reached her bedroom for the killer met her in the hall and murdered her most viciously and brutally, first cleaving her skull with an axe, then slashing her throat from ear to ear with a knife, dragging her body into the dining room where he surrounded it with newspapers, soaked them with paraffin and set them alight.

It seems Elizabeth Harris was the first to smell the smoke. She woke Jane and Eliza and went on downstairs into the dining room, probably because she could not find Emma Keyse in her room. Her employer's mutilated body lay on the floor in a pool of blood, partially burned. Lee then appeared saying he had been woken by the smoke and noise. Elizabeth told him to go to the Carey Arms for help, but he went back upstairs to help Eliza and Jane and then went for the police.

Five separate fires were found, all smelling strongly of paraffin. There was no signs of a forced entry, which meant the killer must have been someone already in the house, or who had access. Although Lee slept in the pantry with only a small partition between that and the hall, he said he heard nothing. The police found the bloodstained axe, and in the pantry a knife covered in blood. It belonged to Lee. Blood was also found on Jane's night-gown from where Lee had helped her down the stairs. He said it was from where he had cut himself when he opened the dining room window to let the smoke out and broke the glass. In those days of course blood tests were unknown...

At the trial he insisted he and Miss Keyse were on the best of terms but curiously enough his step sister said she had heard him threatening Miss Keyse because she had reduced his wages, she said he had shouted, "I'll set the house on fire and watch it burn!" The only obvious suspect, he was charged with murder. The rumours started, most likely when it was found out that Elizabeth was pregnant. One newspaper claimed that more than one person had been involved in the crime. The police ignored such talk. The inquest was held at St. Marychurch on 28 November. On 12 December 1884 Lee returned to Exeter prison to await trial, which began on 1 February 1885. The defence pleaded not guilty on Lee's behalf. They said that as Elizabeth was pregnant then her lover was at The Glen on the night of the murder, thus producing the vehement evidence from her against her brother. Was it possible she was protecting someone? It was a pretty weak defence and of course in those days Lee could not go into the box to defend himself.

On 4 February 1885 the death sentence was passed on him. In some ways it does seem odd that if he was guilty he had made no effort to hide the oil can, the knife or axe. and would have been so inhuman as to want his own sister and the two elderly women to die in the fire? He protested he had no motive and just the loss of 6d a week does seem a rather ridiculous basis for murder.

He was due to be hanged on 23 February 1885. He went on protesting his innocence all the time he was in the condemned cell at Exeter. The scaffold was erected in a small shed like building where a beam held the rope above a trapdoor. Now comes the chief character in this macabre story – James Berry, said to be the best executioner in England! What an enviable title.

Meanwhile the vicar of Abbotskerswell went to see Lee as he waited for the day. He had forwarded a statement to the Home Secretary, Sir William Harcourt, in which Lee alleged some

John Lee

other person was the murderer, but it made no difference.

The macabre part of this story really started the night before the execution when Lee had a vivid dream. Although it was well known he had not been anywhere near the scaffold or the hut in which it stood, in his dream he saw the staircase which led to the area, the scaffold itself, he heard the bolt drawn to release the trap. He said three times nothing happened. He asked that his dream be recorded that day in the Governor's Log and as he walked to the scaffold he knew all the grisly details – the stairs, the very walls leading to the place, exactly as he had seen them in his dream. It was quite impossible he could have seen any of this in the ordinary course of events. The prison bell tolled to tell all of the City of Exeter that Lee was about to hang.

Onlookers crowded the windows. His legs were fastened, the rope adjusted round his neck, the cap put over his head. James Berry pulled the lever, the people watching held their breath, waiting for the sharp jerk, the sound of the snap of the neck bones.

Nothing happened.

Berry pulled the lever a second time. The boards of the trap shook but didn't move. Lee stood calm and unruffled. A third time the lever was pulled with exactly the same result.

The noose was removed from his neck, the cap taken off.

Berry and the warders tried to loosen the trap door, a carpenter was called to make adjustments. All the time Lee stood confident and calm watching the acute agitation of the others. The chaplain intervened and the Governor, the surgeon and the other officials agreed that Lee had suffered more horror than any human being could be expected to survive. He was returned to his cell, through the open window he could see the open grave which had been prepared for him.

And so he went into the record books as the only man in modern legal history to be "hanged" three times and live. It is quite impossible to imagine what such an experience could possibly have been like. The Home Secretary, Sir William Harcourt commuted the death penalty to life imprisonment, which upset some of the friends and relatives of Emma Keyse – they considered the sentence too light.

He was sent to Portland prison in Dorset and eventually released on 18 December 1907. He then returned to Abbotskerswell to live with his mother, enjoying a quiet life; then on 22 January 1909 he married a nurse from Newton Abbot Hospital, Jessie Bulleid. At first they went to live in Durham, and then to London where he worked in a pub in Southwark, in due course they had two children. It was said that he made a lot of money by being put on show at local fairs, and from a film – "*The Man They Couldn't Hang*". Many people took exception to the fact he was making money from having committed murder. Probably as a result of this unpopularity he emigrated to Canada to prospect for gold. During the first world war he joined the Canadian Forces and in 1922 was said to be living in Buffalo, until 1933 when it is believed he died in Milwaukee.

I talked to many people about the different theories for this extraordinary case, one of whom was Mr Lang who then lived in Albert Terrace in Newton Abbot. He told me "When I was a little tacker of about eight I used to do clog dancing and play the clappers. One day down by the Cross Tree in Abbotskerswell as I did my dance, a man came over and gave me half a crown – a lot of money in those days, and my mother said 'That was John Lee, the man they couldn't hang.' His mother was with him and I always remember her hands, one of which rested on John's arm – they were all brown and flabby like stewed pears! It was the thing that stuck in my mind more than seeing him. I suppose as a kid it was because they were so ugly, repulsive."

I think this anecdote by Mr Lang must have taken place soon after Lee was released from Portland for he says he was in early middle age, with a bald head. "A small man, standing looking rather bewildered in front of his mother's cottage."

Mr Lang went on to tell me some of the theories people put forward as to why Lee didn't hang. Some of them I had heard before, some I had not. "They tried a sack of corn exactly Lee's weight on the gallows first and they worked perfectly." "It was like witchcraft, that's all I can say." And talking of witchcraft, Lee's gran lived at Ogwell and was said to have strange powers; she told everyone in the village "They won't hang him." and before sunrise the day before he was to be hanged she left her cottage and set out for Exeter. She walked there and took up her position on Rougemont overlooking the prison. She kept vigil all day, never taking her eyes off it. At evening she tramped back home and the village people firmly believed the failure of the trap to work was due to the power of her spell. When she got home she told everyone "He is safe. I knew they would not be able to harm him."

Lee's own explanation was that the boards of the trap door were swollen due to damp, that the bolts holding the doors were new and opened perfectly with no weight but jammed under pressure.

Another popular explanation is that the lover of Elizabeth Harris was a man prominent in London society who used to slip into the kitchen at night after Miss Keyse had gone to bed and that on this particular night she came down unexpectedly to speak to John who slept in the pantry and when she opened the door saw what was going on, she recognised the man and fainted from shock. That "someone", afraid of a scandal, killed her, started the fire and bribed John with a huge sum of money to take the rap, guaranteeing that with his influence the gallows would not work! Perhaps truth is stranger than fiction; anyway it was said the whole affair caused the Queen so much horror that she refused ever to visit Torquay.

During my research in Torquay library I found a newspaper cutting concerning Isadore Carter, the prosecutor in the case,

Supplement to the Devon County Standard, January 1885, illustrating the Babbacombe tragedy. Views of "The Glen" with portraits of witnesses, officials and prisoner. The accused, 4th row down in centre.

who was said to have told Lee when he came out of prison that the "someone" he had been shielding had died. The story continued that some time during the 1890s two young boys had stood beside their father at an open grave in a local churchyard in Torquay and as the coffin was lowered into the ground containing the body of a young man of high society but insane, that the older man turned to his sons and said "Today they have buried the secret of the Babbacombe Murder."

27

You can still see the place on which The Glen once stood where this incredible story started – Beach Road in Babbacombe. The house is gone but you can look out across the sea where once John's eyes rested, watching the ships, thinking of murder – who knows? Perhaps one day some document will emerge from the mists of the past and reveal all.

Salcombe's First Dark Mystery - May 1975
The Disappearance of Pat Allen

When Pat Allen and her two small children disappeared from Salcombe in Devon during 1975 one of the biggest and most widespread searches for missing persons ever known in Britain was launched – none of the trio has ever been heard of or found.

From the hilltop villa where the family lived Pat could see the yachts bobbing gently on the sparkling blue water of the estuary, for Salcombe is the Jewel in the crown of Devon with its old white-walled buildings, it could even be a town on the Mediterranean. It is difficult to believe anything so sinister could occur against this backcloth; but the disappearance of a mother and her two children remains unsolved to this day. No bodies were found, no one was accused of, or stood trial for murder. Why should they? The case remains open.

Pat loved her flat: Powderham Villa overlooking the estuary

29

For blond, attractive Pat Allen it seemed the perfect place to settle after years of moving from town to town with her husband, John, and two children; in fact she told a friend, "This is the place where I would like my children to grow up." Yet not long after speaking those words, 40 year old Pat Allen vanished from the town. Even more sinister was the disappearance, two days later, of the children, Jonathan aged seven, and Victoria, six. The last known public sighting of the trio was among the peaceful, traditional surroundings of a rural May Day Carnival on Bank Holiday Monday in the neighbouring village of Marlborough.

John, her husband, was the restaurant manager of the prestigious Marine Hotel in Salcombe, much favoured by wealthy yachtsmen, with its four stars, and two swimming pools. According to John he and Pat had an argument during the afternoon of the carnival and when he got back to the flat from work, she was packing her belongings to leave. He said "She drove off in her Volkswagen, leaving the two children behind. Two days later she came back to collect them, saying she was going out of my life forever. I gave her £70 to help her on her way." And that was the last he, or anyone else, saw of the trio. The car was found three months later on the Shadycombe Car Park in Salcombe – it was the police, not Pat's relatives, who started the enquiry.

Money due to her from a Beautician's business had not been collected, a wardrobe of new clothes for herself and the children was left behind; during the time which elapsed after she left, no claims were made for Social Benefit, no places for the children in any schools had been applied for – it was as though they had melted into thin air.

The police distributed 10,000 leaflets with photos of Pat and the two children under the heading "Where are they now?" Every cove and beach in the area was searched, caves into which the tide might carry a body examined. Divers probed the whole of the Devon and Cornwall coastline while an autogiro criss crossed the hills and fields looking for fresh excavations. Helicopters with special equipment to sense shallow graves covered the whole of the countryside round the area. Tracker dogs which had worked in the Sinai Desert for victims of the 1973 war were used. The American Embassy was contacted; there were thousands of responses from the public, but nothing of actual value.

There had been a ray of hope when a jeweller in the north of England handed in a gold necklace with bloodstains, but the Devon police found out that although it actually had belonged to Pat, it was another dead end – as was the report by a lorry driver that he had given a woman answering Pat's description a lift in the north of England. Someone else had seen a similar blond driving a stolen MGB sports car along the North Circular Road – the detailed description tallied exactly with Pat – smartly dressed, well spoken – but again the follow up proved negative.

Twelve months later the National press started to take an interest. The Observer in May 1976, the Daily Mail the following June, and the past history of both Pat and John became known world-wide. Details of the lives of the two main characters were widely circulated. Pat had been born in Keighley in Yorkshire in 1935. When she was 21 she married Marcus Walker, but the marriage only lasted for 12 months. Ten years later she became friendly with an American Air Force Officer and spent some time in the United States and Canada before returning home in 1967. That summer she met John Allen who was then known as Anthony John Angel. In March the following year they married at Halifax Register Office.

It was revealed later that he had left a wife and two young children in Elstead, Surrey, and contemplated suicide at Beachy Head in Sussex; but changed his mind as he swam out in the icy water. He left a suicide note with his clothes on the beach and travelled to the north of England and changed his name. This was when he met Pat Walker as she was then. He was now charged with bigamy and theft, and of obtaining money by false pretences. He pleaded guilty and was given a suspended jail sentence of two years. Pat had sat holding his hand in the court as the sentence was passed. Soon after, they were legally married; their son Jonathan was born in January 1969 and shortly before they moved to High Lane in Cheshire, Victoria was born in May 1970.

John was born in Bournemouth in 1934. Leaving Grammar School he worked in an architects' office, but was restless and wanted to see the world so he joined the Royal Engineers at eighteen, reaching the rank of Sergeant, leaving in 1960 with an exemplary record. He had many jobs and in 1972 was declared bankrupt after an unsuccessful business venture. The family moved to Leicester and for twelve months John travelled in various business projects which often took him away from home and during this time Pat had several men friends in the area; however any differences which might have arisen between John and Pat were resolved and in 1974 they decided to make a fresh start and moved to a caravan site at Dawlish in Devon, where Pat got a job as a receptionist.

In 1975 John went to work as a £50 a week restaurant manager at the prestigious Marine Hotel in Salcombe with excellent references from his former employer at the New Grand Hotel in Torquay. Pat joined him with the children and in March they settled into a flat in Powderham Villa, Devon Road, which was kept for hotel staff. She was a good homemaker and set about re-modelling the kitchen. She made friends with her neighbours in the flat below – Brenda Jones and her husband, Mike, who was a hotel chef.

During this time John became friendly with the attractive and sophisticated Eunice Yabsley whose husband Charlie, had recently died. Charlie was one of the best known charismatic characters in Salcombe and together they ran the Galley restaurant. When he died she had succeeded him as Chairman of the old Salcombe District Council, for he was much involved and admired in public life.

John and Pat Allen had now been in Salcombe for four months when they had a row. Eunice told me this had no connection with their friendship, later John told the police, "The row was simply one of those continuing things between husband and wife. Pat is a wife any man could be proud to walk down the street with, but that doesn't mean that life with her was easy."

On the morning after the May Day Carnival at Marlborough, Brenda Jones had gone up to the flat to ask Pat down for coffee. John was on his own, "Pat's gone away for a few days." Upon which Brenda offered to look after the children but John said his mother was coming from Bournemouth to do so. On the following day, a Wednesday, Brenda said she did see a grey haired lady walking along the road with John and the children and assumed this was his mother. That was the last time she saw the children.

Meanwhile John had asked Eunice Yabsley if she would look after Jonathan and Victoria until their grandmother could do so – however the occasion did not arise as he said his mother had actually turned up and collected the children.

It seems that as a result of this upset John lost his job at the Marine Hotel and it was then Eunice gave him a job at her restaurant, the Galley. Of course at once rumour was rife in the small town. Fanned by the discovery of Pat's Volkswagen in Shadycombe Car Park where it had apparently stood for three months. And then a cousin arrived from Halifax to see why Pat had not written her usual regular letters.

In September the police started their investigations. John was questioned by the CID. What surprised them when John told them his story was that Pat had made so few preparations to leave – the new clothes left behind. John explained this by saying she had only taken the few things which HE had not given her – obviously intending to make a clean break. Then there was the money owing from the Beauty Salon to which she was entitled, not collected. She had made no claim on Social Security for the children, her passport was not valid. Why hadn't he reported her disappearance earlier? He said he

Police frogmen prepare their boat before searching below Salcombe bay.

presumed she had gone off with a boy friend, perhaps to America.

Brenda Jones was interviewed about John's 17ft cabin cruiser which he had often taken them all out in. The enquiries were exhaustive, but John was released.

The press was still having a ball. In June 1976 the Daily Mail ran a headline – "SEA BED HUNT FOR LOST WIFE." They said the Navy was likely to join the nation-wide hunt for vanished wife Pat Allen, aged 40, and her children who had perhaps been thrown into the sea. Detectives had found a small dinghy had vanished the day Pat disappeared, It had been used to ferry the family and their friends to and fro to the cabin cruiser.

The CID had come to the conclusion that Pat Allen had been murdered, then her killer returned to eliminate the children who had probably witnessed the whole affair – but they had to admit eventually they had no shred of evidence. It was in the same month that John Mundy of Basildon whilst on holiday in Salcombe reported that while fishing off Bar Lodge his line had become entangled with a blue handkerchief folded round paper tissues. A piece of flesh was discovered by a fisherman. It was sent to Bristol Forensic Laboratories. Police divers were sent down at once to search the area between Black Rock and Wolf Rock off Salcombe, a grisly task searching for what might be a 12 month old corpse and Group Leader PC Roger Morgan said "The odds against finding anything useful is doubtful, such a corpse would be badly mutilated by crabs." The scandal of this affair shocked and angered the people of Salcombe, mainly because it involved Eunice Yabsley as John was living and working at the Galley. He had repeatedly told the police that he would never have harmed either his wife or children. "I had no motive. I had a good job, a nice flat, why would I want to get rid of my wife and children?" Of course it is reasonable to think that with the memory of John's bigamy, and as a result of the row they had, whatever or whoever it may have been about, Pat thought "Here it goes again. Maybe I'm going to be dropped like a sack of old potatoes," and so decided to take the initiative by not only leaving him but also making conditions as awkward as possible for John.

In 1986 – eleven years after the disappearance of Pat and her children, the then Chief Detective Superintendent John Bisset at the Headquarters in Exeter of the Devon police told me "The file is still open, for months we welcomed information and clues, we used to have people coming forward with hunches every week or so, but eventually the interest dwindled, people forgot. We had co-operation from Scotland Yard, Interpol, Government departments, local authorities, foreign embassies – no stone was left unturned." John himself had written to the American Embassy asking if they could put him in touch with any newspaper or organisation that could help, he even asked a friend who was visiting the US to approach the American organisation akin to our Salvation Army, but there was no response.

Chief Detective Superintendent Bisset told me "In my opinion everything points to the sad fact that mother and children died. We have no shred of evidence to say they are alive – but that is only my opinion. There may be some rational explanation. Pat may be living a normal life somewhere. If so, even after all this time, we appeal to her to contact the police, our only concern is for their welfare, we have no wish to become involved in any way in a domestic affair, but the Force will not rest until the mystery is solved."

It is twenty years ago this May that three members of the Allen family vanished, the children would be in their late twenties. No crime was committed with which anyone could be charged, no bodies found. These people might never have existed except

Patricia Allen

that Eunice Chapman who talked to me so freely is very much alive and living a full life in a small Devon village – a woman who once lived with John Allen. She has written a first class book *"Presumed Dead"*, the autobiography of Eunice Yabsley as she was then, who knew John better than anyone. Pieces of the jigsaw still come to light and one day the Dark Mystery of Salcombe will be solved at last – perhaps....and one of those pieces of jigsaw came to light by sheer coincidence as I was about to send this MS to the publisher, in the shape of a letter from Mrs Josie Coombs of Plymouth.

"Regarding the Salcombe Mystery and Pat Allen and her two children; when my husband worked at Plymouth Dockyard he had an annual holiday from 30 May to 6 June and in 1975 we went to Teignmouth. At the end of the holiday as we caught the train back to Plymouth, walking through the small passage leading from one carriage to another we came face to face with Pat and her two children. She didn't seem in any way upset as they went through into the other coach. I didn't tell the police at the time as I was afraid they might think I was a hoaxer giving wrong information." I asked Josie what her solution to the problem was. "I think the reason they took no money or belongings was because she was going to someone who could provide all this, perhaps an old flame, they may have boarded a ship or plane to Canada or the USA or a private yacht before the hunt for them was on – maybe they were lured into some quasi-religious cult, confident the community would cover all their needs and where they would virtually be anonymous. Who knows?"

Indeed, Josie, who does?

The Maye Murders - June 1936
Triple Slaying at Croft Farm - Kingsbridge

When the famous judge, "Khaki" Roberts was asked to describe what was the most outstanding case of his long career, he replied, "I have no hesitation at all in picking the Croft Farm triple slaying as the most sensational, the most macabre and most baffling case that fell to my lot during my half century at the bar."

At the time he was appearing for the DPP when these horrific killings on the night of 11 June 1936 took place, described as slaughter, set against the peaceful, lush Devon countryside. The family concerned consisted of Thomas Maye aged 71 – a churchman and respected member of the small community where he lived; his wife Emily aged 70 – interested and active in church matters – and their two daughters, Emily Joan aged 28, connected with the local guides, and Gwyneth aged 25, a hockey player and keen rider. They were both unmarried, both deeply involved in all the local social life.

Also living in the house was Charles Lockhart aged 22. He was employed by Mrs Maye as an indoor servant and a gardener. He started work in 1933, his bedroom at the back of the house; one of five orphaned children, he came from Modbury, his father had been killed in an accident at the mill where he worked.

Apart from Tom Maye, Lockhart was the only member of the household who escaped a horrific death on that June night. To outsiders there appeared to be no ill feeling between any members of this rural household.

The sheer horror and unfathomable mystery was made even more macabre by an off-beat twist – indicating the fiendish murderer, in spite of the senseless brutality involved, must have had a streak of compassion for each victim had a cushion carefully placed under their head.

The Maye family had farmed Croft Farm near Kingsbridge in South Devon since 1860 and in this house on the night of 11 June 1936 three women met violent and bloody deaths, and the fourth occupant, the father, received terrible injuries from which anyone less tough would have died.

On the night of 10 June the girls had visited a beach some distance away to help make a film, and didn't return until 3am on the 11th, but in spite of being tired from the late night, the next day the normal routine of the household was carried out.

During the evening Lockhart visited Kingsbridge – Tom Maye had two visitors on business, they left between 8 and 9pm. They saw both girls but not Mrs Maye. No one sensed anything unusual. At 9.30pm Lockhart returned to the farm to fetch a coat as it was raining, he was going to a dance at the nearby village of Stokenham and would not return until late. As usual the back door was left unlocked for him – the door which led into the house from the farmyard, directly into the lower kitchen, the higher kitchen was up two steps and through a doorway. Although at this time he did not see anyone, he heard voices about the house. He would be able to reach his bedroom by a back staircase without going into the other part of the farmhouse, this was quite usual in those days for an apprentice or indoor servant.

He cycled to the dance, arriving at 10pm and stayed until 2.15am, cycling back with a friend as far as the village and then going through the orchard, a short cut to the house where a light was still burning. He put his bike in the barn and went into the lower kitchen, opening the door into the higher kitchen to go up the back stairs to his room. There was a deep pool of fresh blood on the worn stone step, also what he described as a "funny smell". And now comes the first extraordinary fact in this mystery, although I could not find anyone who had queried this in the proceedings. Instead of going to investigate the source of the blood, he turned and ran up the lane, shouting to one of the farm labourers in a nearby cottage,

"Someone's after Farmer Tom! Something's happened up at Croft. Come quickly!" To me this is a second extraordinary fact, again not mentioned, that he should assume Tom was the victim when he hadn't even gone into the rest of the house or seen anybody?

He then went and fetched PC Mogridge who, with two of the labourers, ran back to the farm to discover the wholesale carnage which had occurred. Horror was piled upon horror. Gwyneth was lying in a pool of blood in the doorway leading from the higher kitchen to the foot of the front stairs, a cushion under her head, saturated with blood whilst more blood flowed beside her body. The whole place reeked of paraffin – the "funny smell" upon which Lockhart had commented. Gwyneth's black and white spaniel, soaked in paraffin, stood by the body, licking her face. She was still just alive but

The kitchen door at Croft Farm where Lockhart entered

41

unconscious with horrific head wounds. She wore pyjamas, a dressing gown and one slipper. Near her body lay a walling hammer with a broken handle, covered in blood. Later, at the trial, Lockhart described that he had been using the hammer during the day of 11 June to put up the tennis net, at which time it had been intact. He had put it in the china cupboard under the stairs, although it was usually kept in the roundhouse in the yard. So who but he would have known where it was? Again, no one ever asked this question.

Mogridge went up the stairs into the bedroom at the end of the passage. The bedclothes were on fire, the bed empty and bloodstained. On the landing he found the body of Emily Joan with a trail of blood leading from the bedroom. She was already dead, her head resting on a roll of material to make a pillow, blood was spurting from her head and running down to her feet. Further along lay the missing shaft from the walling hammer. Little did he know what ghastly horrors awaited him

The step from the lower kitchen to the upper showing the step where Lockhart found the blood

as he turned into the main bedroom where the light was on. It was filled with dense smoke which half choked him. In here the sight he saw made what he had already encountered pale into significance.

The double bed was on fire. He saw what he thought was a bundle of rags burning on the floor. Tom Maye lay on the bed, only his head and shoulders were visible, he was covered in blood. And now what Mogridge had thought was a bundle of rags, proved to be the partly burned body of Mrs Maye, her skull smashed in and, as in the case with her daughters, under what was left of her head some soft material had been laid as if to protect it from the hard floorboards.

Over all was the stink of paraffin.

Maye was conscious, he said "Where is my wife?" Mogridge managed to put out the smouldering bedclothes pulling them off Tom. His night-shirt was covered with soot and blood, his feet caked with dirt. In one corner of the room by the door was

A wallhammer similar to the one used in the murder

a pail half full of paraffin. Mogridge replied to his query about his wife, "She sent for me as the house was on fire."

"Where is all this blood coming from?" Maye asked as he raised himself on the bed, "I want to see my wife and daughters." Mogridge told him he would have to go to hospital to have his wounds dressed. Maye then said "Has Lockhart come in? We left the backdoor unlocked. I have been asleep and I do not understand all this blood on the bed." It was then Mogridge made one of the greatest mistakes in police history for he did not caution Tom, but said at once, "What have you done, Tom?" He assumed and accused the man of having committed the murders, which could have been entirely wrong.

At that moment Dr Cowper, the local GP, arrived. Gwyneth was taken to Kingsbridge Hospital where she later died without gaining consciousness. The doctor certified that Emily Joan had only been dead a few hours. Now Maye sitting up in bed, took his watch from under the blood stained pillow, got out of bed and dressed. "It is twenty past five. The men will soon be here to do the milking. Get my wife and daughters. I have a load of manure coming at 8 o'clock." All this in spite of the very deep cuts on his head. It was later proved that under each was a fracture of the skull, each one of which the specialist said would have caused immediate unconsciousness and had been inflicted with the walling hammer. Now, protesting strongly that he had business to attend to, Maye was taken to the Poor Law Institute in Kingsbridge where he talked to the doctors in a perfectly rational manner.

Detective Chief Inspector West of the Devon CID arrived at the farm at 10.45am. It had already been confirmed that there had been no intruder, that nothing had been stolen. The injuries to Emily Joan had been inflicted while she lay in bed, the injuries to Gwyneth would not have incapacitated her and were administered by the murderer while she was standing up facing him... or her... whilst the others had been struck from above and behind, it was the fall downstairs which had most likely rendered her unconscious. Blood and hairs from Thomas, Emily Joan and Gwyneth were found on the walling hammer.

On 12 June 1936 the local press carried the banner headlines:

TERRIBLE WEST CHARLETON TRAGEDY. THREE DEAD. MOTHER AND DAUGHTERS KILLED IN VIOLENT NIGHT STRUGGLE. SECOND GIRL DEAD IN HOSPITAL. POLICE EXTINGUISH FLAMES ON BLOOD SOAKED BED

When all the blood groups had been analysed it was found the crimes could have been committed by an outsider, by Maye himself – or one other member of the household – Emily Joan. Again no one seems to have taken a sample from Lockhart... There was an entire absence of motive. Who would put improvised pillows under the heads of the victims? Paraffin had been brought in from a distant outhouse of which an outsider would have been totally unaware. At the autopsy on Gwyneth the supposition that she was pregnant was dispelled. She had a perfectly normal menstruating uterus.

The newspaper theory was that Mrs Maye was attacked first, that her daughters went to her assistance and then became victims of the murderer.

On 14 July Maye was told he would be prosecuted for triple murder. When he was first told of his wife's death he said "It is awful. She had been in ill health for some time. I was very fond of her. I don't know anything about it, yet I was in the same bedroom. We have all had a very happy time together." Regarding the deaths of his daughters he said, "I don't remember hearing a struggle or shouting. Who was able to do it? Nobody had a grudge against us. Nobody would do us an injury. I think it is absurd making this accusation. I love my wife and daughters too well." And so it was "Khaki" Roberts found himself in Kingsbridge Magistrates' Court with the task of prosecuting Thomas Maye. He said "Since his character was exemplary and there was a complete absence of motive I had to suggest that perhaps some inscrutable trick of the mind had converted a loving husband and father into homicidal maniac. I invited the Justice to say there was a prima facie case against Thomas Maye who, from the state of his feet, seemed to be the one who had made the journey across the yard to fetch the paraffin, and whose hand but his would have placed pillows under the heads of the deceased?

Maye gave his evidence in a cultured voice saying that from the time he went to bed until 9.30am when he found himself in a Plymouth Nursing Home, his memory was a complete blank. "I passed my wife on the stairs as she went up to bed; she put her arm round me and gave me a kiss and a playful punch in the ribs, saying she had some mending to do in the bedroom. I never saw her again. Joan cooked me a poached egg and I went up to bed. I slept pretty well as far as I know. I don't remember the policeman coming in."

He was sent to Exeter Assizes and in his notes Roberts continued, "Mr Justice Charles took his seat in November. I was immediately aware that because of a heavy calendar he continued to deal in a summary fashion with some of the cases on his list, and so it transpired." The Plymouth specialist, Dr Robinson, who had examined Maye, gave evidence that he could not possibly have himself inflicted his terrible injuries, adding that bruises on the jaw were consistent with his having been struck while under the bedclothes. The judge fixed his eye on Robinson saying, "There is no more reason for supposing Maye struck the others than that they had struck him." It was obvious to Robinson he had to throw in his hand and he said, "I will offer no evidence." A verdict of Not Guilty was returned on each of the three charges. Maye stepped from the dock a free man, saying "Thank God that terrible time is over. I knew I would be proved innocent."

So who was responsible for the slaughter on the farm?

The defence never reached the stage of having to tell their theories but there are many fascinating features. Was there a struggle between Gwen and her father on the stairs? Did she collapse, unable to move. Did she fall head first down the stairs and then received the injuries which led to her death. She was the only one who had time to put on her dressing gown and had not been attacked in bed. The walling hammer showed hairs from the other three but not from Gwen. Bare footprints on the floors were those of Joan and Gwen, not of Tom. None of this evidence was ever given.

I talked to Mr Leonard Pedrick of Kingsbridge, the man who was on his way to deliver the manure of which Tom spoke, he knew the Maye family well. "Tom was a man of quick temper, over strict with the girls," he shifted in his seat as he spoke, "and yet I always felt an unhealthy atmosphere existed between himself and his daughters."

How about the witnesses at the trial?

Lockhart gave details of his employment, of the walling hammer which he had used that day to fix the tennis posts, of his return for his coat during the evening when all seemed perfectly normal, and then of his terrible discovery. There was no mention of his remarks about Tom or the fact that he made no investigation of the source of the pool of blood BEFORE running for help. He described Tom as "strong and nimble although he did breathe heavy sometimes and his hands often shook."

Lockhart's friend, Erest William Warren, with whom he attended the dance, was a messenger boy at Kingsbridge Post Office. He said "I saw Charlie during the evening, he was behind me in the Paul Jones, there is no possible doubt he was in the dance hall all evening. We left at 2.10am. It was raining as we rode our bikes. I left him at the school at West Charleton where he jumped off his bike to go through a gateway for a short cut."

William Lambell, labourer, "I was aroused from my bed by Charlie Lockhart who asked me to go to Croft Farm. I couldn't get much information from him as he was very upset. he went to phone the police. At the farmhouse I saw Miss Gwen as I followed Mogridge from the kitchen. She was badly injured and bleeding. Mogridge sent for the doctor."

Thomas Creber, a horseman – "Maye was quick tempered when telling off his men, but soon forgot the incident. On Thursday 11 June I was working horses in a field at 3pm and Maye came to speak to me about work. I saw nothing unusual in his manner. At 5.30 I took the horses back to the yard. Maye was milking and feeding the pigs. I went home, went to bed and slept until I was knocked up at 3.30am. I dressed and went to the farm."

Charlie Lee, labourer who had worked for Maye for 20 years. "I never knew him get into a violent temper, but he did sit and brood when in trouble. He didn't talk much and was very tight with money."

William Steer – "On Thursday I was called to Croft Farm in my capacity as vet to deliver a calf. At 6.45pm I went to a field where Mr Harvey, who worked for Mr Maye, was with the cow. Later I went to the back door of the farm and Miss Maye answered. It was 8pm. She told me her father was home but busy with a Mr Smith. I waited in the garden and later Mr Maye came and talked to me about business and general matters. I have known him for 20 years and saw nothing unusual in either his, or Miss Maye's behaviour."

Mr Smith was an accountant from East Allington – "When I arrived to see Mr Maye he was in the yard and appeared perfectly normal. We carried out our business and I said good night. The whole time he was at ease and no different from usual."

Walter Farr, wheelwright and carpenter of East Charleton – "I have done a lot of work for Mr Maye during the last 30 years and always been on the best of terms, a very decent man to deal with, but I had noticed lately he had got shaky and irritable. A month ago I was repairing some hurdles for Mr Cornish when Mr Maye came and talked about some work he wanted me to do. I made arrangements to call and see him that evening. At first he seemed pleased with the arrangement, then suddenly he flared up and said, 'It appears you are ready to creep up Mr Cornish's backside!' I was greatly surprised as previously he had been very pleasant. I said, 'You mustn't come over and bully me like that,' he started to walk away and said, 'Are you going to do the work or not?' So I said 'no.' I have seen him twice since but we did not speak. I had been very upset. As he left he said 'If you were a younger man I should feel like hitting you,' and I replied 'If you do I shall have you in the Town Hall.' "

Miss Duffy, the matron of the Cottage Hospital in Kingsbridge said "On 12 June at 5.20am Miss Gwen Maye was admitted in a very collapsed condition and unconscious. Her face was almost unrecognisable, covered with dried blood. There was a strong smell of paraffin. She had on pyjamas and a dressing gown. Both arms were blue and contracted, her feet were very dirty. She died at 8.20am without regaining consciousness."

Detective Chief Superintendent Bisset is retired now from the Exeter police, and told me he was too young to remember the actual murders, but as stated earlier, he said the case was always held up to young constables as an example of how NOT to conduct a murder enquiry. Mogridge had not cautioned Maye and virtually accused him on the spot by his words "Tom, what have you done?"

Thomas Maye lived in a nearby village with his married daughter for many years after the murders. Mrs Maye and her two daughters were buried in West Charleton churchyard. In March 1938 the farm was sold to the Rogers family who still live there. Mrs Rogers showed me over the house and it is virtually unaltered since that terrible night, even the built in cupboard where the walling hammer was placed still stands, and the worn depression in the kitchen step where Gwen's blood had formed a pool.

At the time of the sale an observer remarked, "The house was neat and clean, the grass on the tennis court needed cutting..." The tennis court where Lockhart had used the walling hammer, the last time it was used before it became a murder weapon. He is perhaps the most intriguing character in the whole ghastly business, probably mainly because we know so little about him and can only surmise how he fitted into the household. He was an indoor servant employed by Mrs Maye, not the usual farm apprentice who would have been answerable to the "maister". He would even perhaps have been as close as a son, a woman involved in many good works, he came from an orphanage so perhaps he was one of her protégés. Could he have been in love with one of the girls? One thing is certain, we shall never know what bubbling cauldron of emotion, passion, jealousy may have seethed beneath the peaceful appearance of the religious and highly respected family. The more any avenue is explored, the further off seems the solution.

West Charleton churchyard where Mrs Maye
and her two daughters are buried.

The Warcombe Farm Tragedy, Kingsbridge
June 1904
Two Young Farmers – One Murder, One Suicide.

This murder is outstanding for two facts – firstly because the acts themselves were both witnessed by a boy of five years old who described them in such clear terms that the coroner said he could have been a man of mature years. Secondly, the father of the murderer tried to make much of the fact that his son had been stung by a viper nine years before, and on each anniversary since, his face had gone into spasms so uncontrollable that he turned away so people could not see. In addition it was a double tragedy involving two young men – one murdered and the other who committed suicide. Some of the description of the double tragedy is best quoted verbatim from the newspaper, a supplement to the Kingsbridge Journal and Salcombe Times dated 18 June 1904, which opened thus:

> "Kingsbridge and the surrounding district were shocked on Saturday evening by the intelligence that a murder had been committed at their doors, and still more when it learned it was a double tragedy. Until a late hour the main street was crowded by persons who were stunned by the affair whilst numbers walked out to the scene of the tragedy"

So what was the cause of this furore in the peaceful district of the beautiful South Hams where all seemed tranquil and idyllic.

> "This first indication of trouble was when Mr Edward Friend, a horse breaker of Ledstone near Kingsbridge clattered at great speed on his chestnut mare down Fore Street. He reported to the police that an awful tragedy had taken place at Warcombe Farm, two miles from the town. A lad who was a farm apprentice named Albert Corner aged 20 had been paid off by his employer Mr Hubert Baker aged 28 and had taken terrible revenge and shot him dead. Corner had then cleared off taking the gun with him. Sergeant Yendell from Kingsbridge rode with all speed to the scene."

Artist's impression of Warcombe Farm, and plan.

52

(Later it appears, on his bicycle as the account says he was a first class bike rider.) He had also alerted his colleagues PCs Greenslade and Rowland. Dr L de Courcey Harston had already arrived on the scene to find the victim dead. Then the search for Albert Corner, the murderer, began – a man with a violent temper at large with a gun. However they didn't have far to search for in a field not 100 yards from where he had shot Baker, lay the body of Corner having apparently shot himself. The account continues:

> "Mr Hubert Baker was well known and respected in the district – a bright gentlemanly young fellow following the profession of farmer which he dearly loved. Ten minutes before he died he had spoken to his neighbour's wife, Mrs Perrott, and little Wilfred Perrott aged 5½ who went with Mr Baker to drive some bullocks into a fresh field and thus became the eyewitness to the tragedy."

Corner was the fourth son of a tanner, William Corner, living at Goveton, the family having come from Mid Devon. He had had several jobs on local farms but –

> "in consequence of his bad temper and surly manner he was unable to get on with his fellow workmen or keep a situation for any length of time. He had been in the employ of Mr Baker for six months, previous to which he was in the employ of Mr Luscombe of Rake, the adjoining farm. It was because of his lazy habits and surly manner that Mr Luscombe had dismissed him."

Mr Baker's widowed sister, Mrs Cummings, kept house for him and he was so attached to her that he had declared to his friends that he should not marry as long as his sister remained with him.

> "He had not paid any attentions to any lady although rumour was spread to the effect that he was engaged. It is not known that Mr Baker had an enemy except this unhappy youth who took his master's life while under the influence of an evil temper. Mrs Cummings had never liked Corner, feeling he would do some harm in one of his tempers, as it had turned out. He was 5ft 7in tall with a bulldog type of countenance."

It seems that Baker had to reprove Corner several times and gave him a month in which to mend his ways. At the end of the month he had promised to behave properly, but the trouble came to a head on the Friday after dinner. Mr Baker was shearing some sheep while Corner.. 'idled nearby'. Looking at his watch Baker said "It is five to two and time you went after the horses." An angry reply came and then some swearing came from Corner, he picked up a crowbar and threatened Baker with it. After a moment he cooled down and went about his work although Baker told him he would definitely have to leave at the end of the month. Later he told his sister what had occurred and she begged him not to wait for the month but to pay him off at once. This he did on the Saturday afternoon.

Corner went upstairs and packed his tin box after tea. Later Mr Baker was taking some cows into a field while his sister did the milking. With Baker was the five year old boy, Wilfred Perrott. As they crossed the field the boy suddenly called out to Mr Baker and pointed to the hedge, "There's Albert with a gun!" Mr Baker turned round. Before any warning could be uttered with a shout of "You b...... ," Corner fired from a range of a few yards. The charge struck Baker's face with fatal effect. He shouted out to his sister, "Annie... oh... oh..." How he managed this is surprising. He fell, but managed to rise again, running 40 yards down the hill pursued by Corner who had jumped off the hedge and fired again, hitting Baker from behind in the shoulder. The farmer fell dead. The little boy, who was unhurt, told his story very clearly saying that Corner appeared to take no notice of him when he ran through the gate to tell Mrs Cummings what had happened. She had heard the shots and rushed to the stables and begged Mr Friend and young Wellington, who was with him, to see what had happened. When they found the body, at first they thought it was an accident, Friend got on the hedge, shouting at Corner to come back. ""Come back Albert, do you know what you've done? You've killed your maister!" There was no reply and he said to Wellington, "Whatever's the matter with the boy, is he mad,

54

what is he doing, is he shooting the cattle?" There were two more shots as he spoke. Having put the body on a hurdle they went for medical aid and the police, and Mr Friend galloped into Kingsbridge. Sergeant Yendell who was an excellent cyclist rode to the field and with PC Greenslade found the body of Corner with his face and head blown away. The gun was between his legs with the muzzle towards his head and his right hand gripped the stick which he had torn from the hedge and by the aid of which he had fired the trigger (cp the Winkleigh murders).

"The police found the tin box which Corner had packed, lying about 30 paces from his body. Flattened grass on top of the hedge showed where he had lain in ambush. The gun was the property of Mr Baker and kept in the pantry in the house – the cartridges on the kitchen mantelpiece. Hundreds of people visited the spot on Sunday, the police did their best to restrain their morbid curiosity and there were no unseemly incidents."

Apparently on the Monday an enquiry was held with Mr Kellock, the deputy coroner in charge. The main feature of this was the remarkably clear and straightforward manner in which little Wilfred Perrott aged 5½ gave his testimony. Mr J S Perrott, his father, held the little boy between his knees as the boy spoke:

" 'I was with Mr Baker on Saturday evening when I went to the field with the bullocks. I saw Albert shoot Mr Baker. I saw Albert up on Mr Luscombe's field hedge with the gun, and go out over. Albert fired the gun at Mr Baker and I saw him bleeding from the face. I saw Albert fire the gun a second time. He got off the hedge and ran after Mr Baker and shot while both were running. I saw Mr Baker fall down the first time after Albert fired and then got up and ran away towards the gate, and fell down where he was found. I saw Mr Baker bleeding and he had to walk with his head down....' "

It seems that here a juryman interrupted with a question and Mr Kellock said the little boy was giving evidence splendidly, let him alone to tell his own story. The child continued, "After

55

Mr Baker fell down the second time Albert ran back through the hedge and into the next field. I ran down to tell Mrs Cummings what had happened and met her coming up."

Mrs Cummings told how Corner had said to her brother "You and your sister ought to be dead, you are two b......s."

She said she was milking the cows when her brother left to drive the cattle and he told her through the window of the shippon "It's all right now, Albert is clear, gone, and his box with him and you need not be afraid." She explained the gun had been in the larder on Saturday afternoon when she cleaned the floor, so Corner must have come for it after he left the house with his box, while she was milking.

William Henry Corner, Albert's father, said nine years ago to the very day the murder occurred, Albert had been bitten by a viper and every year it could be noticed a twitching occurred on his son's face, although if he thought anyone was looking he turned away. There was nothing else peculiar about him. The coroner remarked that the bite of a viper would not have any effect after nine years. He then went on to remark on the fact that the gun and cartridges had been easily available and should be a warning to everyone about such dangerous weapons being left about. There were frequent cases of men in fits of temper destroying themselves and others.

The verdict was that Albert Corner was guilty of wilful murder and then committed suicide, at the time being of sound mind – felo de se.

Perhaps the saddest part of this story of all is that Albert Corner, murderer and suicide – was buried at West Alvington at 10pm at night by lantern light. The vicar, Rev T Bell-Salter read a short portion of the burial service and a grave had been prepared at the head of the churchyard under a tree close to the hedge – presumably this was considered unconsecrated ground suitable for such a criminal. Mr Mundy, the Relieving Officer had made the arrangements for this as the parents refused to accept responsibility...

Who can say whether they were responsible or not for the boy they had given life to and the way they shaped that life from the day he was born.

West Alvington Church where Albert Corner was buried